WE ARE BUILT FOR THIS

FOR THIS

Sheila Latimore

Table of Contents

Preface

Before you took your first breath, before your heart beat its first rhythm, God knew you. He saw the path you would walk, the mountains you would climb, and the storms you would endure. Jeremiah 1:5 reminds us of this truth: "Before I formed you in the womb, I knew you; before you were born, I set you apart..." This declaration is not just a statement. it is a promise. It is the foundation of understanding that you are not here by chance. You are built for this. This book is a testament to that divine design. It is a journey through faith, perseverance, and the unyielding strength that God instills in each of us. Life, with its twists and trials, is a canvas painted with both joy and struggle. Yet, through it all, there is purpose. Every setback is a setup for something greater, every trial a testament to resilience. We Are Built For This is more than a title.it is a proclamation of faith. It is the recognition that God's hands have shaped your destiny with precision and intent. Through these pages, you will encounter stories of triumph over adversity, faith that moved mountains, and courage that stood firm in the face of fear. My hope is that as you read, you are reminded of your own strength, your own purpose, and the God who walks beside you every step of the way. No matter the obstacles you face or the challenges that arise, know that you are equipped, you are empowered, and you are purposed. You are built for this

Acknowledgement

First and foremost, I want to thank God—the Father, the Son, and the Holy Spirit—for granting me the wisdom and courage to write this book. I am deeply grateful to my daughter, Santana Latimore, for always standing by my side as my unwavering supporter. My heartfelt thanks go to my sisters, Earnestine Derico and Brenda Stovall, for their constant belief in me and their encouragement to keep moving forward. I also want to express my deepest gratitude to my late mother, Classie Jones, whose words of wisdom inspired me to strive for excellence in all things. Finally, I extend my sincere appreciation to my church family, friends, and colleagues for their support and prayers.

In advance, I want to express my heartfelt thanks to everyone who embraces the messages within this book. I pray that God opens your eyes to His Word and grants you the understanding He desires for you to receive.

We Are Built For This

We are built for this! Do you understand that God has already equipped us with all of the necessary tools we need to not only survive but to thrive in this lifetime? How? Because God has given us gifts, talents, and treasures for us to complete our mission. These tools were placed in us long before the world began.

In Jeremiah, God said he knew us before we were ever formed in our mother's womb (Jeremiah 1:5); meaning, God had a conversation with us while we were in heaven, explaining to us the tasks and duties we are to complete while on earth. There is a volume of the book that is written about each of us in heaven. We are built for this because Jesus had already paid the price through shedding his blood on the cross. When Jesus died for our sins, he connected us back to God. He bridged our relationship back to God through the shedding of his blood. We are now able to go to God to communicate and find out how, what, when, and who we need to connect with to complete our mission and how to effectively use our gifts, talents, and treasures to assist on Earth and ultimately, in the Kingdom of God.

We are built for this because we know who we are. Whatever we say will come to pass, because death and life are in the power of our tongue. Understand that you are the righteousness of God through Christ Jesus. We do not have to wait until we get it right to come to God. Once you give

3

your life to God, he begins his work on you. Come as you are and allow God to clean and sanctify you through his love, word, fasting, and prayer. God created us to implement, design, produce and to flourish on earth (Genesis 1:28). We are built for this because we possess all of the God given attributes to accomplish all endeavors needed to perform to his will. Do we possess the confidence to step outside of the boat, into the deep to begin our tasks? Do we surround ourselves with people who have already accomplished what we desire to complete?

"For we are his workmanship, created in Christ Jesus unto good works, which God hath before ordained that we should walk in them."

Ephesians 2:10 (KJV)

Life

We are built for this because God has given us life more abundantly (John 10:10). Life will always be full of haters, who sit back watching, as you rise to the top. Please do not let people hinder or stop the plans God has instilled in your heart. Life is meant to be well lived.

Following the principles, ordinances, and commandments of God will carry you a long way. Life is filled with opportunities just waiting for you to walk through that door. Believe in yourself and do as God commands you. Obey God with all of your heart and love everyone as if they were you. Stop waiting around expecting people to bless you; instead, use the gifts, talents, and treasures God has given you to obtain wealth, both spiritually and, perhaps, monetarily. Put your hands to work doing whatever it is you determine to be sufficient, and watch God bless you. Do not waste time talking negatively about others, but use your time to become the best version of yourself! Life is not about what happens to you. Life is about how you handle and respond to what happens to you, no matter how big or small, favorable or unfavorable. Will you speak of life or death? Will you trust God, or will you trust man? Will you compromise or rise to the challenges of life? Will you play a game of chess or checkers? In life, sometimes you will be the ensample, meaning at times you will be preaching the word, while you are going through the calamity. In life, you may be the example, meaning, at times, we have already gone through what you are preaching about.

The Bible is our basic instruction manual which guides us on how we are to love God and treat one another. We often lean on our own understanding instead of trusting God's word and teachings in certain areas of our lives because we are scared, especially when we have never had to rely on Him before; however, at this point in our life, it's in our best interest to ask God to help our unbelief and get beyond our fears.

As anecdotal evidence of what God can do, as long as you believe and have 100% bought into his doctrine, here is a personal testimony I want to share: After falling three months behind on my mortgage, I received a foreclosure notice in the mail. I prayed and praised God for making a way out of no way. At the time, I was working as a full-time substitute teacher. I applied for a loan and I remember being so excited because the loan was approved. Do you remember that old commercial that said, 'if you want a tough stain out, shout it out?' Many times, in my life, I praised God like it was already done. When you praise God, He sets up the ambush against your enemies 2 Chronicles 20:22). Please read 2 Chronicle 20 in its entirety. After they praised God, all their enemies turned against each other and killed themselves off. The only thing Judah, Jehoshaphat, and his people had to do was collect the spoils, riches, and precious jewels, which took them three days; therefore, praise the Lord when you are in difficulty and challenging times. Choke the devil out. Why do you say that, Sheila? I am glad you asked, laughing out loud. Genesis 49:8 states "Judah, art thou he whom thy brethren shall praise; thy hand shall be in the neck of thine enemies; thy father's children shall bow down to thee." I want you to catch this golden nugget. Judah stands for Praise, in other words, your hand is already on the enemy's neck! Praise God and watch God work it out for you.

God has not given us the spirit of fear; however, he has given us power, love, and a sound mind. I am now going to give you three occasions in my life when I just had to trust God. When my husband James passed away in 2002, I told God, "I know you are not making me a widow at the tender age of 30." The doctor looked at me and said, If I bring him back, he will not remember me or our daughter. So, with tears in my eyes, I said, "God, not my will but thy will be done." At that moment, his spirit left his body, and I felt his presence around me.

The second occasion was when I asked God, "Please help me, because I was used to having a slice of the pie anytime I wanted." God kept me; he did not let me fall. Now I want to keep it clean so that you understand where I was coming from. God kept my heart and my mind throughout this experience.

The third occasion was my calling to become an elder. Keeping it real, I was like, sure, talking to myself. My sister Brenda told me when I was 19 years old, I would be preaching the word of God; Brenda told me I could not run from God. In my mind, I said, oh yes, I am doing a good job. I always thought I would come to God when I was old and gray, but how many of you already know that God has a different plan? I said when I am blind, crippled, and crazy, that is when I am coming to God; however, I found myself giving my life over to Jesus Christ when I was 25 years of age on December 25, 1996. This has been the most exciting, interesting, and fulfilling thing I've ever done in my life. Life is about learning how to live in the purpose, anointing, and calling of God while developing into the best version of our creator that we can become. We are God's workmanship, built to bless and glorify his name. Many said it is hard to live this Christian life, but my Grandmother always said "Anything worth having is worth fighting for." Imagine if Christ had said, giving his life for us was too hard, or I cannot do it. God gave us his all, so we should give him our all, not just during busywork. In gathering the harvest, be a soul winner. Being a soul winner by going into the hospitals, nursing homes, jobs, and families, exemplifying, reaching, and teaching that the kingdom of God is at hand. God created me to be a leader, so why am I settling to become just an employee? Why am I settling for less than what God has given and instilled in me? One thing you have not discovered is going back to your creator and asking Him to help you perfect the gifts, talents, and treasures that He has placed in you.

You allowed yourself to be comfortable where you are. Look to the parable of the ants. In the summer and fall, they are storing up for the winter season. In other words, ants are diligent workers in the two seasons where we are enjoying and relaxing, instead of working to get ahead. Like the ants, we must prepare ourselves for this journey and be willing to put in the work to reap the harvest. We must be willing to plant and water and trust God to do the increasing through multiplication 30, 60, or a hundredfold. Simply, we must be witnesses to people through the way we live and by giving back to the people in our community. For example, if you see I am hungry, get me some food, or teach me how to fish, so I can possess the skills to survive on my own. Life is about making the hard right, instead of the easy left. Life is not about letting everyone know what you are doing. The Bible says, "Do not let the left hand know what the right hand is doing." Do not let people know what you have been called to do; position your hands to do it, and they will know when God has completed it within you; He will make it known. Everyone is a leader in the order of functioning, so we have to respect each part. In the body of Christ, God has given us, apostles, prophets, evangelists, pastors, and teachers. Why did God give these positions? He gave us these positions to improve, refine, and empower the saints to become proficient and equipped in God.

"And God blessed them, and God said unto them, Be fruitful, and multiply, and replenish the earth, and subdue it: and have dominion over the fish of the sea, and over the fowl of the air, and over every living thing that moveth upon the earth."

Genesis 1:28 (KJV)

Leadership

We are built for this because God has called us to be ambassadors for Christ. You become a leader when you decide you've had enough of being led astray. There aren't too many people who want to lead because they want to be liked by everyone. A leader stands out and receives resistance because of their expectations. A leader is meant to lead, direct, be a lightning rod for descension and opposition, plus guide you down the right path for you to glean from and grow. I remember serving in the United States Army at my first duty station, Fort Bragg, or PT Heaven, laughing out loud. While serving, I had a sergeant who would always get in my face every week and belittle me while yelling at me; this went on for three years. I never said a word to her because, God said, be quiet, go get a Coke, shake it up, and drink it. I did exactly what God told me. When I got ready to deploy to Korea, that same sergeant told me, I knew you were a real Christian because you never said anything or talked about me. Sometimes, we have to let people see God in you by example or by walking the walk. Leadership can make the scariest person one of the bravest. Leadership can transform followers into great leaders because the leader determines the follower's destiny. A leader knows each of their follower's skills, abilities, and accomplishments; therefore; he or she can place that follower in a position that will advance them to the next level - putting them in a position to be the most successful. God gives us shepherds after his own heart. For example, take Gideon in Judges 6, when the Lord called him a mighty man of valor. Of course, Gideon did not think so; he said, I am the least in my father's house, meaning, I am the lowest. Gideon had the Lord prove himself by allowing the fleece to be wet one day and dry the next. He did this to make sure it was the Lord who was talking to him, and he saved Israel (Judges 6:36-40). Everyone is not meant to go with you on your journey, so they will leave, or you will have to cut them loose (Judges 7:5-7). Gideon had 32,000 people with him. God said, "Tell the ones who are fearful and afraid to go back!". 22,000 left, which left only 10,000. God said, still too many people take to the battle against the Midianites. Gideon took the 10,000 left down to the river to get a drink of water; God said, whoever laps the water with his tongue as a dog laps, set them by themselves. When finished, they only had three hundred, which means 9,700 men were sent back. And the Lord said unto Gideon, "By the three hundred men who lapped will I deliver the Midianites into thine hand, and let all the other people go every man unto his place." A leader can motivate a group of people to come together for the good of a common goal. The blind cannot lead the blind. Even though someone has a title, they can still be blind? Do not be impressed with a title or calling. Ask the following question:

- Where are we going?
- What is your vision?
- How do you plan on accomplishing this vision?

Why is leadership essential and vital to the body of Christ and organizations?

Leadership is important because of the following:

- Change does not happen without leadership.

- Development does not happen without leadership.

- Improvements do not happen without leadership.

- Correction does not happen without leadership.

- Advances do not happen without leadership.

- Maturity does not happen without leadership.

- Success does not happen without leadership.

People are being led each day, whether it is directly or indirectly. Many times, as leaders, we stand out for the following reasons:

- We make the policies, strategies, and procedures.

- We break traditions or do not follow traditions.

- We do not tolerate or compromise what we

believe in or stand for.

- We challenge others to come from their position of comfortability to a level of discomfort.

What is the difference between leadership and management?

Leadership is the ability of an individual to influence, motivate, and enable others to contribute to the organization's success. The role of management is to control a group or group of individuals in order to achieve a specified objective.

Management is responsible for controlling an organization, a group, or a set of entities to achieve a particular objective. Managing is about making sure the day-to-day operations are being performed as expected. A leader communicates in order to set direction, inspire, and motivate the team. Leadership requires a vision to guide change. Whereas managers focus on achieving organizational goals through process implementation, such as budgeting, organizational structure, and staffing, leaders are more concerned with thinking ahead and seizing opportunities. It is possible to be a manager and a leader at the same time. But keep in mind that just because someone is a great leader, doesn't mean they'll be a great manager.

Things That Leaders Are Concerned About

They are built for this because they are visionaries at heart. Leadership requires a vision to guide change. A leader is one who always takes the initiative and invests a great effort to accomplish the company's vision. If you are leading others, you must lead from the front. These are the four things that leader does:

- Empower People

- Inspire People

- Lead Change

- Shared Vision

Leaders are always examining where their organization stands, where they want to go, and how they can reach the goal by involving the team. On the other hand, leaders are more concerned with how to align and influence people than how to assign work to them. As a leader, one might question and challenge the authority to reverse decisions that may not be in the best interests of the team. A leader personally invests in tasks, projects and demonstrates a high level of passion for work. Leaders take a great deal of interest in the success of their followers, enabling them to reach their goals to satisfaction. Effective leaders are adept at fostering a positive work atmosphere and building trusting relationships with their team, which results in high engagement levels and reduced turnover rates. A leader's capacity to hit performance benchmarks and realize organizational objectives can also be used to gauge their efficiency. The six traits a leader possesses are the following:

- Vision

- Honesty

- Integrity

- Inspiration

- Communication Skills

- Ability to Challenge

There is a leader in each of us according to the gifts and talents we possess. It is up to the individual to decide whether or not they are ready to lead another or continue to be a follower. Either way, it is up to that individual to plan which one he/she wants to be.

"And when they began to sing and to praise, the Lord set ambushments against the children of Ammon, Moab, and mount Seir, which were come against Judah; and they were smitten."

2 Chronicles 20:22 (KJV)

Marriage

We are built for this because marriage is a commitment made before God, which holds the man and woman to their vow of being together, until death do them apart. Can a man and a woman mutually love each other without boundaries or limits? I believe, as long as you put God first, he will make the marriage an easier institution to navigate. Man is the head of the household and needs to be respected, loved, and appreciated throughout marriage. Men must learn to love their wives, as Christ loved the church and his children. Men should be the provider, protectors, and hold providence over the household; on the other hand, women are the helpmate, providing essential counsel, support, caretaking and homemaking, among other duties. Look at the man, as the head and women as the neck. Women are built to support, uplift and expand a man's visions. As women, we are nurturers above all else. We are the one person our husband confides in and trusts with all his heart. Our job is to cover him in prayer and train the children up in the Lord, not just by word, but through our actions and interaction with each other. Wives, submit to your husband if he's in Christ because if he is in Christ, he's not going to tell you anything that harms or destroys the trust or the household. Wives must love, respect, honor, and submit to their husbands. I know submission in today's society is a dirty word to some, if not most. Actively listen and come to an agreement with the understanding that submission is for the common good of the household. Even if the roles become reversed and the wives become the breadwinners, please still love, honor, respect, and cherish his mindset and openness. Do not belittle him; still treat him like the king he is and deserves. I am speaking from experience because I was the breadwinner in my marriage; however, I always treated him like the king that he was. I used the word "Was", because he is no longer here with me – he is with the Lord. I would always do these few things once a week:

- Run his bath water.

- Have date night once/twice a week.

- Make sure his dinner was ready before going to different services or places.

- Clean his hands and feet.

- Always spent quality time with him, speaking into his life.

- Always sitting rubbing on his head, hands, and back, letting him know how much I appreciated him

Yes, we had our share of issues like any other couple but we learned not to discuss anything with each other when we were upset. The reason was, we loved and respected each other enough not to want to say something that would cost the other any regret or pain. Marriage is about learning how to continuously love, learn, grow, pray, improvise, compromise, sacrifice, forgive, and forget. I got married at the age of 21 and never had a regret. My husband passed away on August 2, 2002. I was still in love with him. Our daughter is 33 years old now and doing well, thanks, be unto God. Another thing, my husband was not saved when I met him; he was not even going to church. Through God showing me and teaching me how to do the following for Him before I left to attend any church service:

- How to conduct and carry myself before

- Still love, respect, and honor by having everything in order before attending service or going to various places

- Teaching not to argue about everything, pray

- Anointing his head every night

- Continuous praying for his soul

- Anoint the collards and cabbage greens.

My husband gave his life over to God a few years before he passed. He and I would pray with each other and for each other. My husband lived without kidneys for six years. Do not put family members, friends, siblings, spiritual leaders, or anyone in your business but God. The cases I am talking about are if he drinks or smokes, that stays between you and God. Pray and watch God deliver him and set him free. In some situations, you must talk to someone, such as in cases of mental, physical, or emotional abuse; a baby outside the marriage; and adultery. It would be best if you sought some type of counseling.

"Who can find a virtuous woman? for her price is far above rubies. The heart of her husband doth safely trust in her, so that he shall have no need of spoil."

Proverbs 31:10-11 (KJV)

Love

We are built for this because love covers multitudes of sin. Love is a word that has many different levels; however, it seems to have narrowed down to just mere words. Love is one of the major ingredients in any relationship that holds or bonds two individuals together. A woman is built to nurture and care; it is her God-given design. So, it should be no surprise that whatever you give us, we multiply it. There are four types of love:

- Eros

- Philia

- Storge

- Agape

Eros love is the sexual or romantic type of love. It often involves being sexually or physically attractive to someone. This kind of love by itself can cause great joy or great sorrow depending on the situation at hand. It is not enough to sustain, maintain, or manage a relationship.

Philia is a brotherly and sisterly type of love. This is the kind of love that is extended to a friend or lover. This is a healthy relationship between sisters, brothers, and friends. Knowing that one is loved and wanted is an essential part of survival. Everyone wants or desires to feel loved by someone.

Storge is the love that a parent has for his or her child. This love goes beyond boundaries to instruct, correct, direct, and lead our children on the right path. Training and raising children in the fear and admiration of God and loving them through all situations while praying and holding them accountable for their actions.

Agape is loving mankind the way that God loves us. God does not look at our outward appearance of what we are wearing or look on our face; however, God looks at our heart. God sees past the smiles and fine clothing; he stares into the very soul or essence of who we are now and shall be in the future. I often find myself asking God, "How can I love mankind the way that you love them?" God gave me the simple answer: love and treat everyone as you would yourself. Sometimes we seem to think more highly of ourselves than we should, but remember our righteousness is a filthy rag. It is Christ who died for every one of us.

When you love others as you do yourself, you will do the following:

- Forgive them quickly.

- Restore them in meekness.

- Pray for them continually.

- Give of time, money, and gifts as God directs.

- Teach them by being a living example and

example for them.

- Sit down and have a conversation to get to know those who labor among you.

- You would not be so quick to judge or criticize someone else.

- Stop backbiting and being a busybody.

- Encourage and exalt

- Challenge walk worthy in vocation or area in which you are called

Do not just say you love me in words, but your actions are far from reality. Love is the key, that ingredient that is needed today. It's not about receiving money, houses, or land; it is about gathering the harvest that is waiting on us. When was the last time you reached your hand out to give to others or help someone else? I ask that question because some people think church is only in the building. I want to challenge your thinking to propel you to look beyond the church building. Ministry is just serving, and serving must go out beyond our individual church building. So how can we minister to or serve others well? Laugh out loud. I am eager that you ask. We can serve others through the following:

- Part of the outreach ministry in your church

- Part of the missionary department in your church

- Giving of your time, gifts, and talents when needed

- Going to the nursing home to visit the elder

- Going to the hospital praying for the sick

- Giving away clothes, food, shoes, and essential needs to the less fortunate

- Preparing A Meal for the Sick and Shut-In (only the ones that cook)

- Volunteering to help with youth

- Helping to clean your local church

- Continuously Praying

- Carrying the Word of God to others

- Volunteering to teach the youth and adults Sunday School/Bible Study

- Part of the Usher Board

In other words, whatever you can find your hands to do, complete it with all your heart, mind, body, and soul as unto God.

"Beloved, let us love one another: for love is of God; and every one that loveth is born of God, and knoweth God.
He that loveth not knoweth not God; for God is love."

1 John 4:7-8 (KJV)

A Call To Salvation

Romans 10:8-10

But what saith it? The Lord is nigh thee, even in thy mouth, and in thy heart: that is, the word of faith, which we preach;

That if thou shalt confess with thy mouth the Lord Jesus, and shalt believe in thine heart that God hath raised him from the dead, thou shalt be saved.

For with the heart man believeth unto righteousness; and with the mouth confession is made unto salvation.

Dear Lord Jesus,

I know that I am a sinner, and I ask for Your forgiveness. I believe You died for my sins and rose from the dead.

Today, I turn from my sins and invite You to come into my heart and life. I make You my Lord and Savior.

Help me to walk in Your ways and grow stronger in faith each day.

In Jesus' name, Amen

About the Author

Sheila Latimore has faithfully served as an elder in the House of God since 2012. She is both an educator and a veteran, with a deep passion for children and the elderly. With over sixteen years of experience in education and eight years of service in the military, her life has been marked by excitement and challenges that, with God's guidance, she has been able to overcome. Born and raised in Montgomery, Alabama, she is the second oldest of six siblings.

In We Built for This, the stories shared are living testimonies of the author's own life experiences. This book is designed to inspire, uplift, and encourage those on their Christian journey to keep pressing forward and never lose faith in God. Every trial we face becomes part of our testimony and ministry. We are called to work out our own salvation with fear and trembling— understanding that, as Christians, we must live out our faith with deep reverence and humility, trusting that it is God who strengthens and empowers us.

www.ingramcontent.com/pod-product-compliance
Lightning Source LLC
Chambersburg PA
CBHW051252120626
46547CB00014B/1906